GNAT

123 South Broad Street, Mankato, MN 56001, USA

Printed in Italy

Art Director: Rita Marshall

Book Design: Stephanie Blumenthal

Text Adapted and Edited from the French language by Kitty Benedict

Library of Congress Cataloging-in-Publication Data

Benedict, Kitty.

Gnat/written by Andrienne Soutter-Perrot; adapted for the American reader by Kitty Benedict; illustrated by Monique Felix.

Summary: Discusses the physical characteristics, life cycle, and usefulness of gnats.

ISBN 1-56846-041-4

1. Gnats—Juvenile literature. [1. Gnats.]

I. Soutter-Perrot, Andrienne. II. Felix, Monique, ill. III. Title.

QL467.2.B465 1992

595.77'1--dc20 92-7666

WRITTEN BY

ANDRIENNE SOUTTER-PERROT

ILLUSTRATED BY

MONIQUE FELIX

CREATIVE EDITIONS

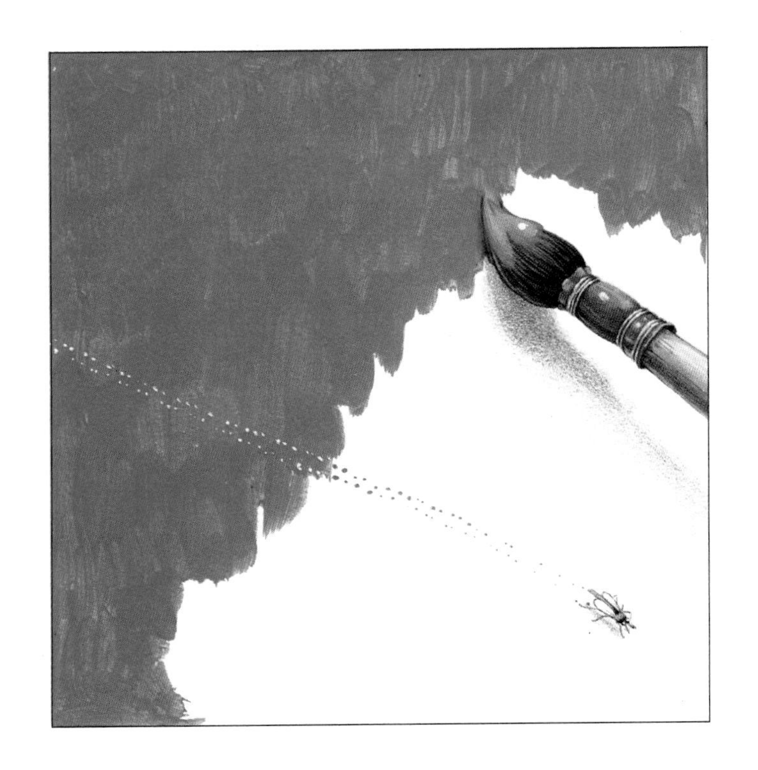

WHAT IS A GNAT?

A gnat is a very small fly.

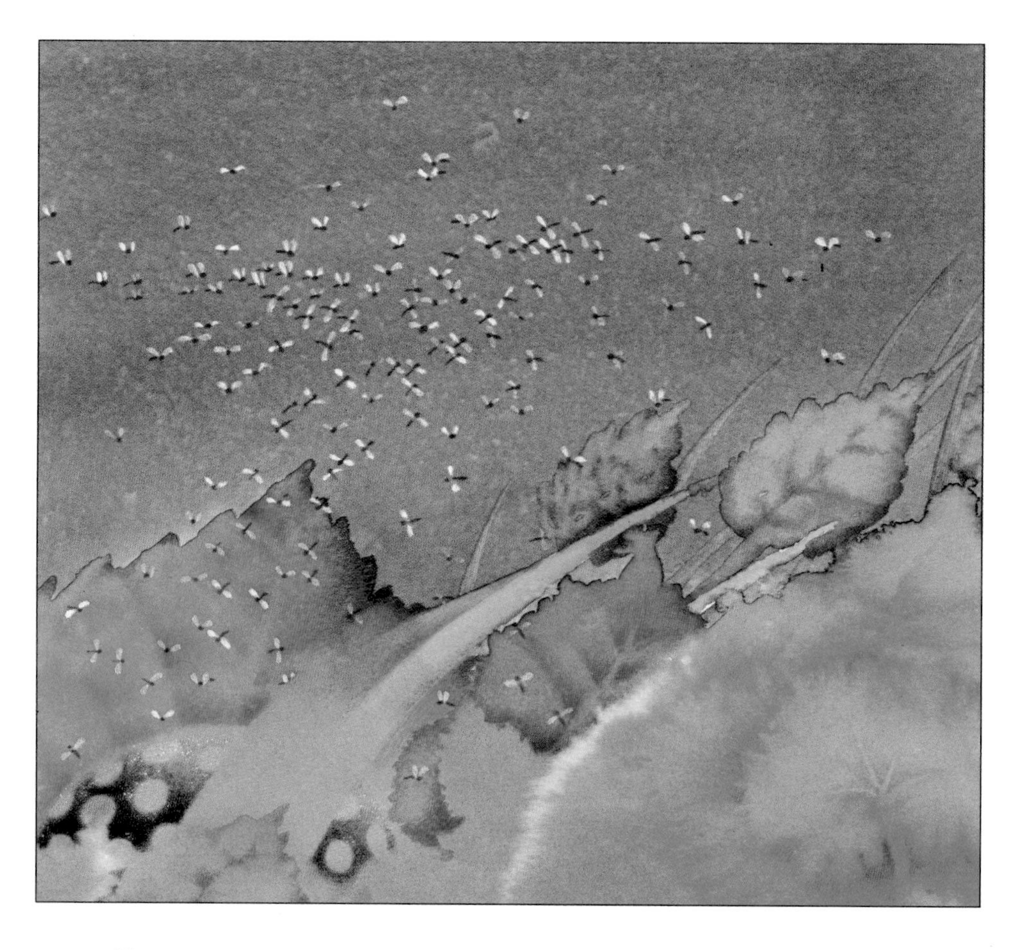

Gnats are so small that we hardly notice them, except when they swarm together in a little cloud.

Gnats are also very light—so light that if one lands on your nose, it barely tickles.

Gnats have no special color. They can be gray, light brown, yellowish, or black.

Even so, they eat, breathe, move, and have young, like we do.

A gnat belongs to the animal kingdom.

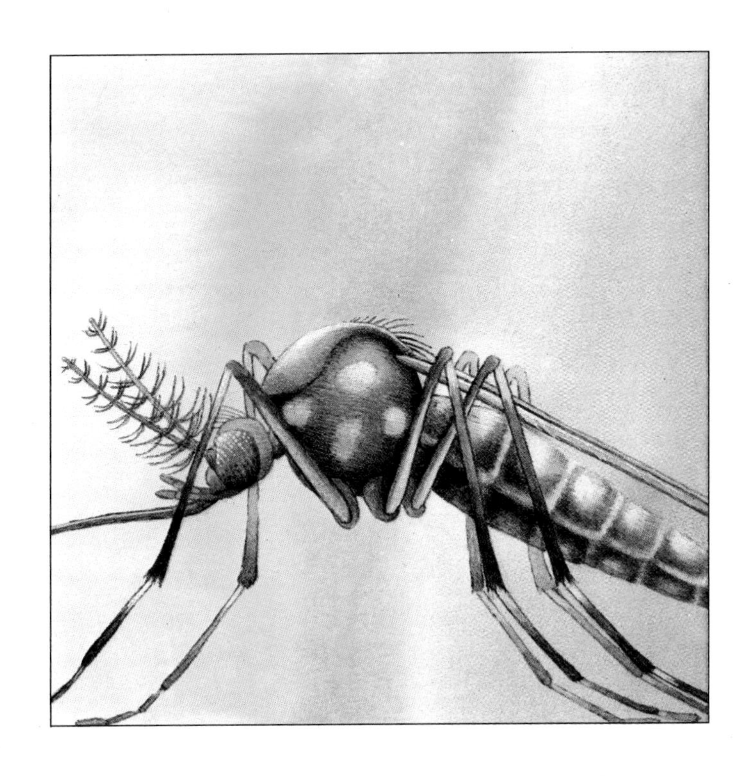

WHAT DOES IT LOOK LIKE?

The gnat's body is divided into three parts: the head, the thorax, and the abdomen.

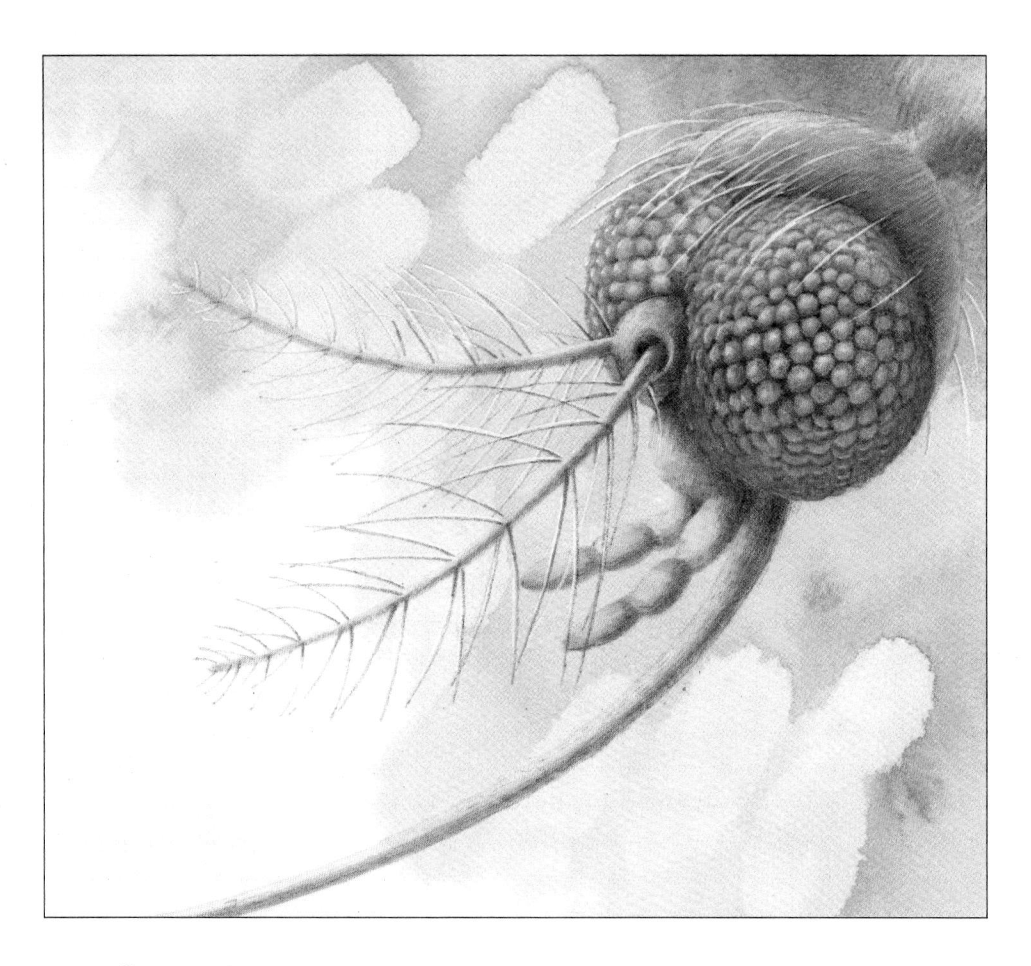

On its small, round head are two huge eyes, two antennae, and a long tube, the proboscis.

The gnat smells odors with its antennae and sucks food with its proboscis.

Attached to the gnat's thorax are two transparent wings. When the gnat flies, the wings flap so fast they make a buzzing sound.

Six hairy legs grow out of the gnat's thorax. The legs have sticky tips, which explains how gnats can walk anywhere and even rest upside down.

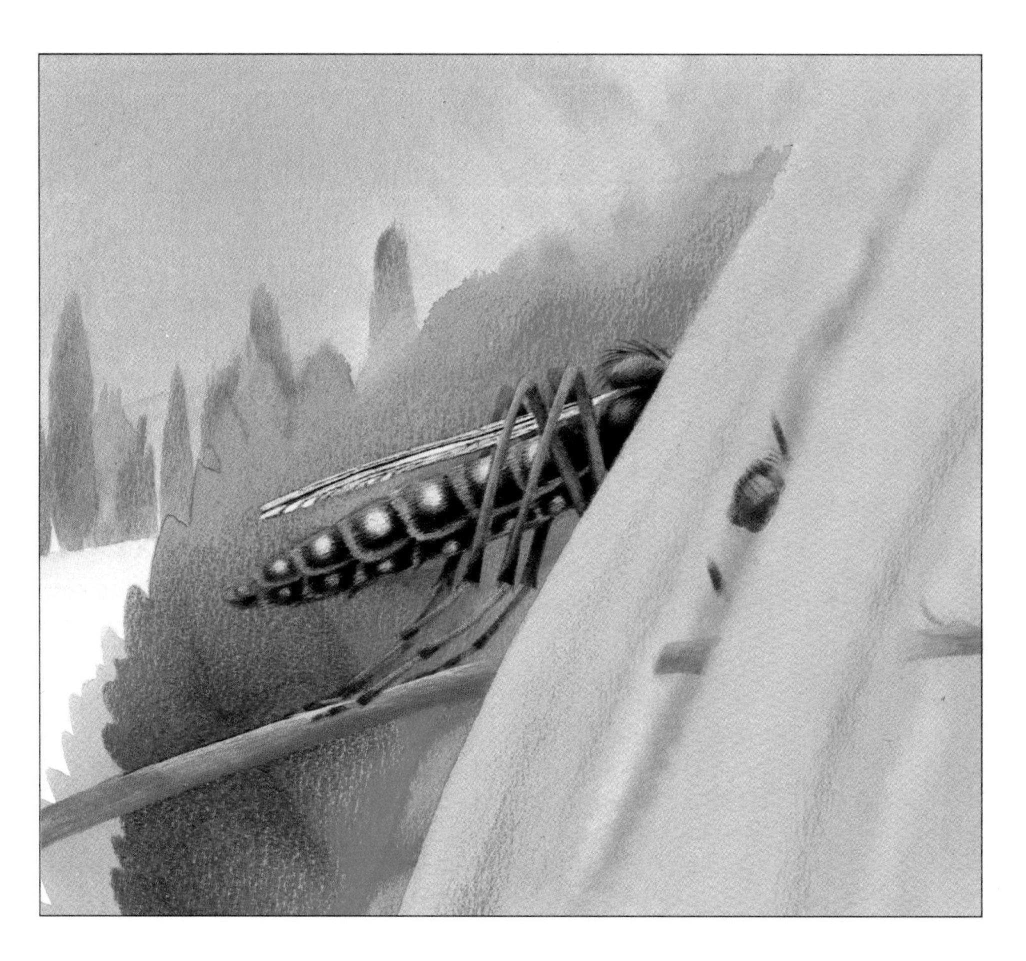

The third part of the body, the abdomen, is long and narrow. It contains most of the organs.

The gnat is an insect.

WHERE DOES IT LIVE?

Gnats may lay their tiny eggs on moss, mushrooms, or dead wood.

Sometimes a gnat pierces a leaf and lays its eggs there. Then the leaf forms a gall, or lump, around each egg.

But most gnats lay their eggs on stones or plants at the edge of a pond. The eggs dangle in sacs beneath the water's surface.

The young that come out of these eggs look like little worms. They are called larvae, or maggots.

The larvae swim and squirm and crawl around, eating all the time. At this stage, they cannot fly at all.

The ones hatched on land feed on dead leaves, ripe fruit, plant stems, and grains of wheat.

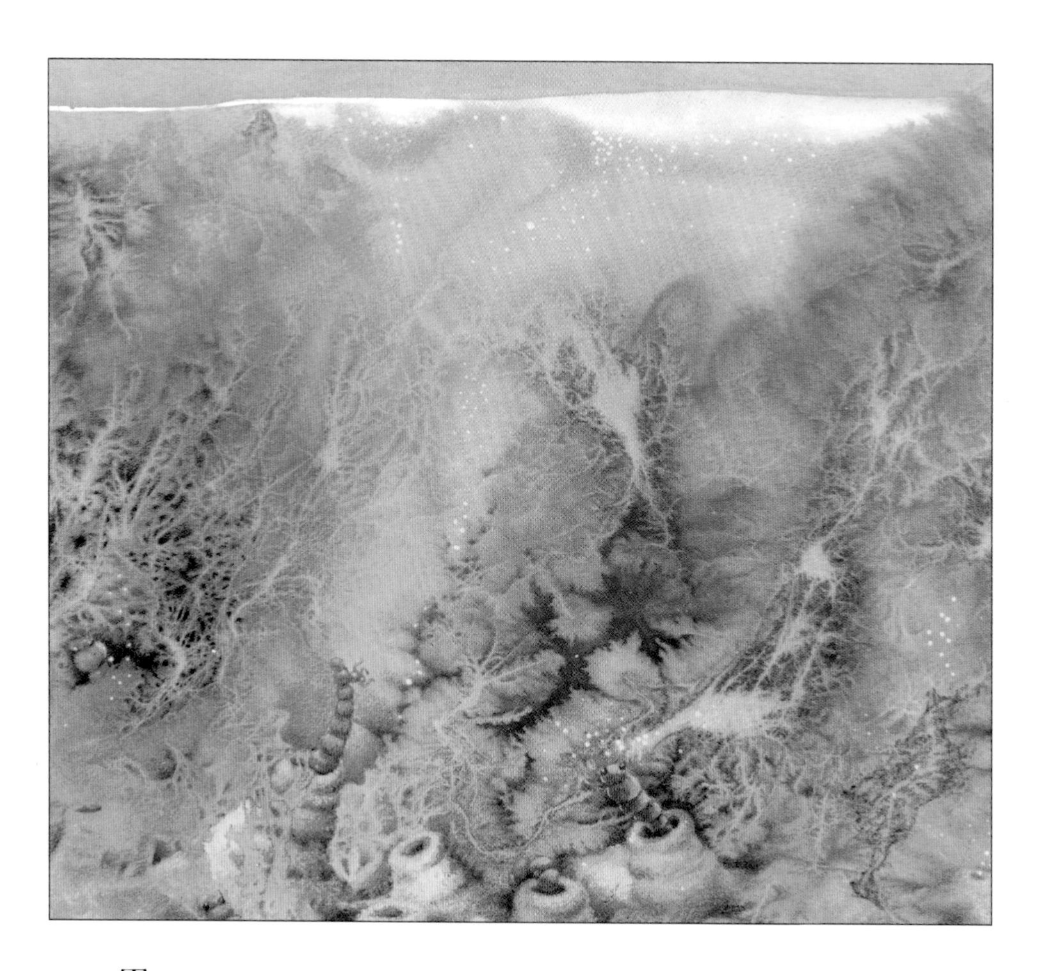

The ones hatched in water burrow into the silt and feed on algae or microscopic animals floating by.

The larvae grow very fast. Soon they stop eating, and their skins harden into shells. They become pupae.

Inside their shells, the pupae stop growing, but transform themselves completely. This amazing process is called metamorphosis.

Finally each pupa's case breaks open and out flies a winged gnat.

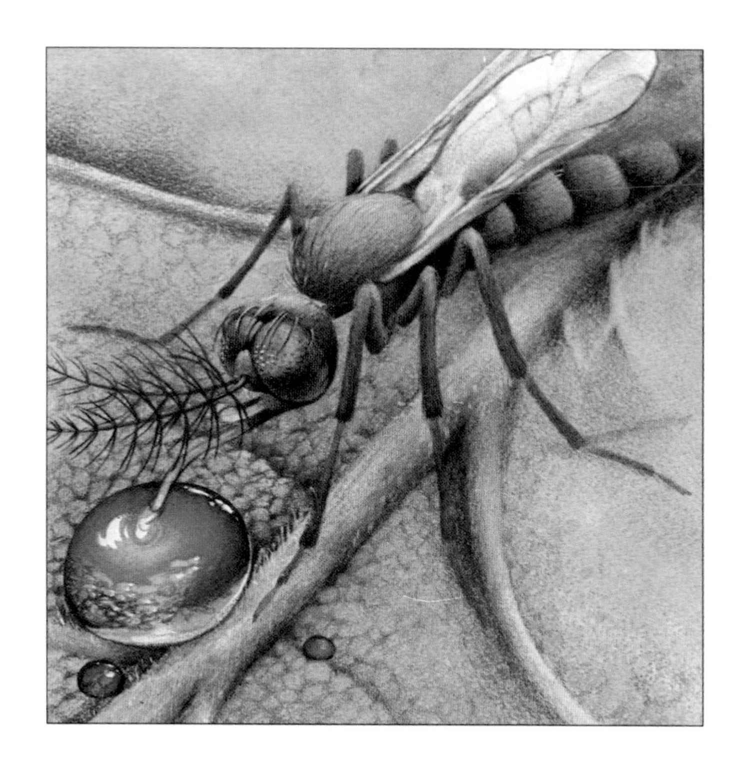

WHAT DO GNATS DO?

Gnats hardly eat at all. A few tiny droplets of liquid are all they need to live.

But gnats are prey to many other animals, such as insects, fish, frogs, and birds.

Swallows eat nothing else, in fact. They catch gnats while flying through the air.

If there were no more gnats, there would be no more swallows. Then who would tell us that spring is here?

Even something as tiny as a gnat is important on Earth.

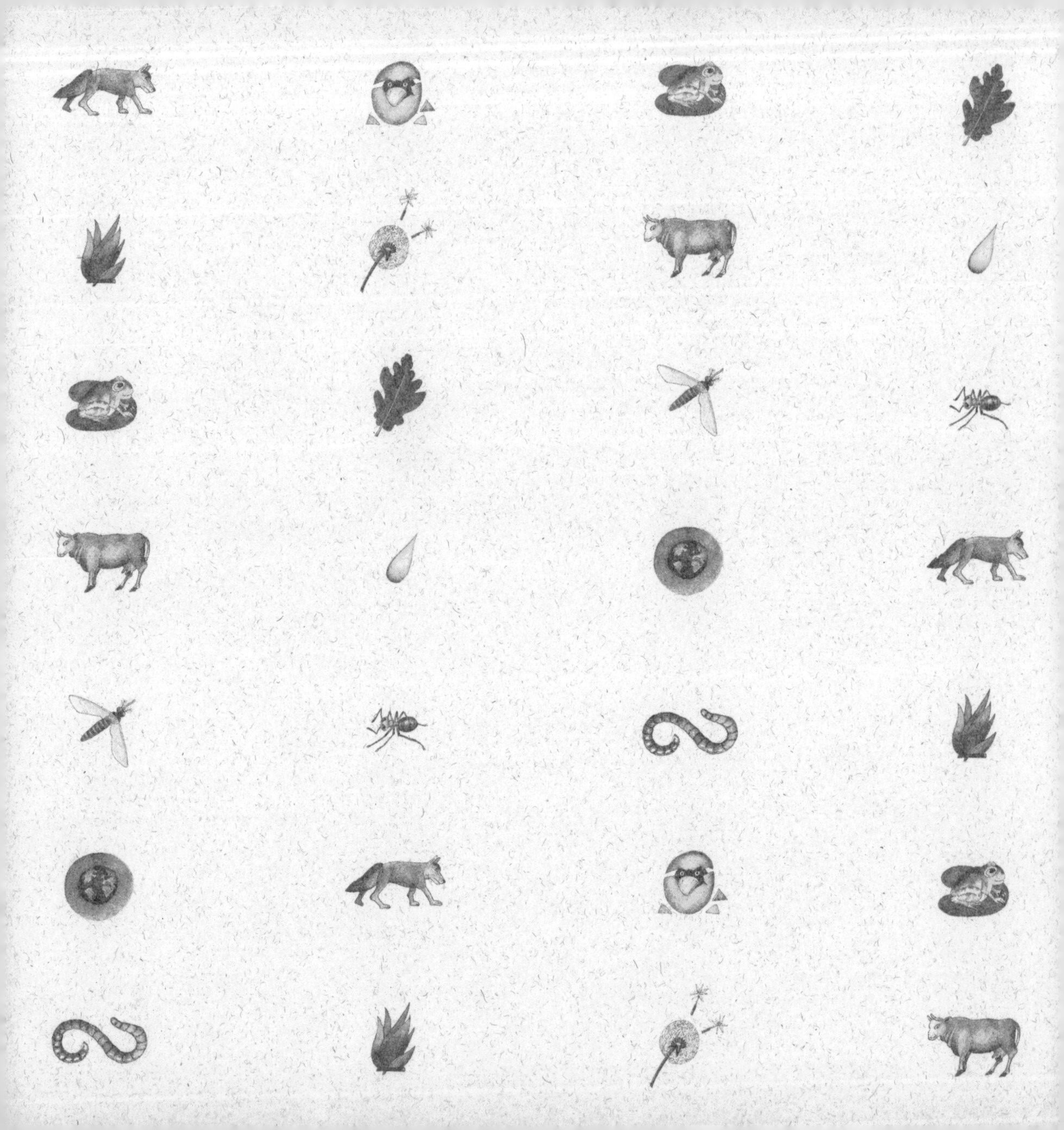